P9-CWD-860

BARACK
OBAMA
COLORING BOOK

GARY ZABOLY

DOVER PUBLICATIONS, INC.
MINEOLA, NEW YORK

Planet Friendly Publishing
✔ Made in the United States
✔ Printed on Recycled Paper
Text: 50%   Cover: 10%
Learn more: www.greenedition.org

GREEN EDITION

At Dover Publications we're committed to producing books in an earth-friendly manner and to helping our customers make greener choices.

Manufacturing books in the United States ensures compliance with strict environmental laws and eliminates the need for international freight shipping, a major contributor to global air pollution.

And printing on recycled paper helps minimize our consumption of trees, water and fossil fuels. The text of *Barack Obama Coloring Book* was printed on paper made with 50% post-consumer waste, and the cover was printed on paper made with 10% post-consumer waste. According to Environmental Defense's Paper Calculator, by using this innovative paper instead of conventional papers, we achieved the following environmental benefits:

Trees Saved: 14 • Air Emissions Eliminated: 1,278 pounds
Water Saved: 6,156 gallons • Solid Waste Eliminated: 373 pounds

For more information on our environmental practices, please visit us online at www.doverpublications.com/green

Note

On January 20, 2009, Barack Obama became the forty-fourth president of the United States of America—and its first African-American head of state. In this coloring book, you will learn about Barack Obama's historic journey from his childhood in Hawaii to his inauguration on the steps of the Capitol building in Washington, D.C.

Your first stop is Kenya, Africa, where Barack's father grew up. Next, you will find out how his parents met. On the pages that follow, you will discover where Barack lived, what he studied in school, why he became involved in politics, and even how he met his future wife, Michelle. It's an exciting journey, and as you learn about President Obama, you can also color in the pictures and make his story come to life.

Copyright

Copyright © 2009 by Dover Publications, Inc.
All rights reserved.

Bibliographical Note

Barack Obama Coloring Book is a new work, first published by Dover Publications, Inc., in 2009.

International Standard Book Number
ISBN-13: 978-0-486-47320-8
ISBN-10: 0-486-47320-1

Manufactured in the United States by Courier Corporation
47320103
www.doverpublications.com

Barack's father, Barack Obama Sr., was born in 1936 in Kenya, Africa. He was the son of a farmer and a member of the Luo people. Eager to educate himself, he wrote to colleges in the United States. The University of Hawaii offered him a scholarship. Here, by the shores of Lake Victoria, he reads the acceptance letter from the university.

After arriving in Honolulu in 1959, Barack Obama Sr. studied economics at the University of Hawaii. It was here that he met a fellow student, eighteen-year-old Ann Dunham from Wichita, Kansas. They married in 1961.

Barack Hussein Obama Jr. was born in Honolulu, Hawaii, on August 4, 1961.
Although his parents separated, little "Barry," or "Bar," had a happy childhood.
In addition to the love and care he received from his mother, he was deeply
cherished by his mother's parents, Madelyn and Stanley Dunham.

3

Barry's parents divorced in 1964. His father returned to Africa to take part in the growth of Kenya, which had become an independent nation. His mother remarried, and Ann and Barry moved to Jakarta, Indonesia, the home of Ann's new husband, Lolo. There, Barry enjoyed spending time with the family's animals, including several baby crocodiles!

At his new school in Jakarta, Barry wrote an essay for his first-grade class entitled, "I Want to Become President." Later on, in third grade, he wrote another essay, "My Dream: What I Want to Be in the Future," again declaring "a president."

When the family moved to a better neighborhood, Barry attended a different elementary school. But his mother decided that her young son would be better off returning to the United States, and she sent him back to Hawaii, where, in 1971, he moved in with his grandparents. A year later, his mother, along with Barry's half-sister, Maya, joined them.

Towards the end of 1971, Barack's father came to America from Kenya to visit. Barack Obama Sr. gave his son a basketball and a recording of Kenyan music for Christmas. Barack Jr. grew to like and respect his long-absent father, but, unfortunately, this was the last time that Barack would see him.

Barack's mother returned to Indonesia to continue her college studies. Barack was a good student. He also excelled in basketball, becoming a star player at school (he is shown here taking a jump shot). The team won the state championship in 1979, Barack's senior year. As a teen, he sometimes experienced racism, and he began to discover his bi-racial identity.

Barack moved to Los Angeles, California, in 1979 to attend Occidental College. There, he found himself surrounded by many more African-American students than in Hawaii. He began to think about racial issues, human rights, and politics. He gave a speech on campus about the oppression of blacks in South Africa.

In 1981, Barack transferred to Columbia University in New York City. All around him, he saw the difficulties facing the minority residents of Harlem, such as unemployment and poor living conditions. He worked at a construction job to pay for expenses but focused his efforts on studying for a degree in political science.

At the age of twenty-one, Barack Obama graduated from Columbia University. He held several jobs in the financial and consumer fields. Still interested in working in the area of civil rights, he pondered his future. However, when he learned of the deaths of his father and a half-brother in motor-vehicle accidents, he began to seriously consider his direction in life.

Barack decided to move to Chicago to join the Developing Communities Project. It meant a cut in pay, but it also meant taking on a job that would make a difference in the lives of many poor, struggling people. He loaded up his car and drove from New York to Chicago, with a new sense of purpose.

On a walking tour through some of the most economically deprived sections of Chicago, Barack saw the ruins of factories that had once employed thousands of people. He also encountered run-down apartment buildings, and citizens whose problems with unemployment, poverty, and crime were troubling realities.

Politicians and community leaders could not agree on how to solve the problems of Chicago's disadvantaged communities. Barack Obama used his insights, education, and persuasive voice to offer ideas and to organize community members. He supported programs that helped people find jobs, get better housing, and make their voices heard by voting in elections.

Realizing that a law degree might enable him to better serve the community and, perhaps, enter politics, Barack decided to go to law school. He chose Harvard University—where his father had attended graduate school. But first, he planned a long-desired trip to Kenya, his father's birthplace. There he met many relatives, shown above, and made connections to his African heritage.

Barack and his half-sister, Auma, went on a safari. He saw lions, elephants, hippos, and wildebeest, and was deeply moved by the majesty of Africa's wildlife and unique landscape. He also visited the graves of his father and grandfather, where he cried, wishing that he had their guidance in life.

Returning to the United States, Barack began his studies at Harvard Law School. He wrote articles for the *Harvard Law Review* and was also its editor. In 1990, he was elected as the *Law Review*'s first African-American president. People began to take notice of Barack Obama, and he was soon regarded as a rising star in American politics.

While a student at Harvard, Barack took a summer position with a Chicago law firm. It was there that he met Michelle LaVaughn Robinson. Born in Chicago on January 17, 1964, Michelle was also interested in the law, and had attended both Princeton University and Harvard Law School. She was the attorney who was appointed to train Barack at the law firm. In the course of working together, they grew to like each other, too.

After graduating from Harvard in 1991, Barack moved to Chicago to both practice law and to teach at the University of Chicago Law School. He and Michelle Robinson became closer, and, in October 1992, Barack and Michelle married. They are shown here with their mothers at the wedding.

Barack never lost sight of his political ambitions, and, in 1995, he ran for the office of Democratic state senator from Illinois. By knocking on doors and introducing himself, he was able to tell voters about his plans to address the problems in their communities, and he won the election.

During the last month of his state senate campaign, sadness entered Barack's life. In November 1995, his mother died. Her illness was made worse by high medical costs, and Barack realized that he needed to help others find health care they could afford. He used his political office to introduce laws about health care into the senate.

Malia Obama, Barack and Michelle's first daughter, was born in 1998. In 2000, Barack ran for Congress. But he was not successful this time, as his opponent was better known, and he was defeated. Barack was very disappointed at this setback.

Barack's disappointment did not last long, for his family was overjoyed with the birth of their second daughter, Sasha, in 2001. The next year, he won a third term in the Illinois state senate. Now he set his sights on running for the office of Illinois representative in the United States Senate. Barack Obama won the election with seventy percent of the vote, and the Obamas moved to Washington, D.C. He was sworn in as a U.S. senator on January 4, 2005.

Barack had impressed many people with the speech he gave at the Democratic National Convention in 2004. Now, as a senator, he was taking part in events at the national level. He joined the Senate Foreign Relations Committee and traveled to Europe, the Middle East, and Iraq, widening his knowledge of foreign policy issues. He is shown above in Moscow, Russia.

Barack published his first book, *Dreams from My Father: A Story of Race and Inheritance*, in 1995. In 2006, he brought out another book, *The Audacity of Hope: Thoughts on Reclaiming the American Dream.* By now, he was known for his way with words and his powerful speeches, and politicians began to wonder whether Barack might run for president someday.

On February 10, 2007, Barack Obama stood before the Old State Capitol building in Springfield, Illinois—where Abraham Lincoln had given a famous speech a century and a half earlier—and announced that he was running for president in the 2008 election. More than ten thousand people came out on that bitterly cold day to share the historic moment with Barack and his family.

Barack was up against a very strong field of Democratic candidates for president, especially Senator Hillary Rodham Clinton, the former First Lady. But Barack Obama's energetic campaigning and effective use of the Internet spread his message and raised donations in a way that had never been done before. The enthusiastic support of TV superstar Oprah Winfrey boosted his popularity with many Americans.

In order to persuade Americans that he was the best candidate to address the issues troubling the nation, Barack used campaign slogans such as "Yes We Can" and "Change We Can Believe In." As he participated in debates, addressed the media, and traveled around the United States, meeting voters and listening to their concerns, he constantly used the theme of change.

The Democratic National Convention took place in Denver, Colorado, in August 2008. After winning the most delegates, Barack Obama was chosen as the Democratic party's presidential candidate. He asked Joe Biden, Democratic senator from Delaware, to be his vice-presidential running mate. Barack debated his Republican opponent, Senator John McCain of Arizona, and the nation watched expectantly as the race drew to a close. On November 4, 2008, Barack Obama became the first African-American President-Elect. He is shown with his family at Grant Park, Chicago, where Obama supporters had gathered to celebrate Barack's election.

On January 20, 2009, Barack Obama was sworn in as the forty-fourth president of the United States of America. With his hand on the Bible that the sixteenth president, Abraham Lincoln, had used for his swearing-in in 1861, Obama was administered the oath of office by Supreme Court Chief Justice John Roberts. The televised event was seen by people around the globe, including the village in Kenya where Barack Obama's father was born.